In the social circumstances of the 1920s, it was almost inevitable that the young Louis Mountbatten and Edwina Ashley would meet and fall in love. He was directly descended from Queen Victoria and numbered most of the crowned heads of Europe amongst his friends. She was beautiful, intelligent and fabulously wealthy.

Yet, behind the glamour and success, they were two very different personalities. As Dickie pursued a glittering career, Edwina lived a life that was wild and bohemian.

Unconventional though it was, theirs was a love that ran deep. In a letter to Edwina in 1927, Dickie wrote: 'You see my sweet, you happen to be my first, principal and truest friend. That is why I love you so.'

Hulton-Deutsch Collection

Popperfoto

OF FAME AND FORTUNE

BORN WITHIN A YEAR OF EACH OTHER, BOTH DICKIE AND EDWINA INHERITED A LIFE OF PRIVILEGE. IN THE GILDED SOCIAL CIRCLES OF 1920, THEIR MUTUAL ATTRACTION WAS IMMEDIATE

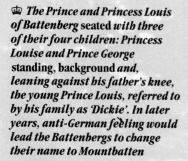

♛ *The Prince and Princess Louis of Battenberg seated with three of their four children: Princess Louise and Prince George standing, background and, leaning against his father's knee, the young Prince Louis, referred to by his family as 'Dickie'. In later years, anti-German feeling would lead the Battenbergs to change their name to Mountbatten*

T HE FUTURE LORD MOUNTBATTEN, BORN AT 6 am on 25 June 1900 at Frogmore House, was described by his mother as 'a most vigorous baby who came kicking and screaming into the world'. Shortly after hearing the news of his birth, his infirm great-grandmother and godmother Queen Victoria drove round to see the new arrival. 'He is a beautiful large child,' she pronounced approvingly. Indeed, she desired that such a healthy specimen be called Albert, after her beloved and long-dead husband.

The baby was duly christened His Serene Highness Albert Victor Nicholas Louis Francis Battenberg three weeks later. But shortly afterwards Queen Victoria died and he became known as Nicholas – shortened to 'Dickie', to avoid confusion with his royal relative the Tsar of Russia, whose nickname was 'Nicky'.

Dickie's early childhood was bathed in a golden glow. The fourth and last child of Prince Louis of Battenberg and Princess Victoria of Hesse (Queen Victoria's granddaughter), he was the youngest of the family: George, his brother, was seven when he was born, and his sisters were 10 and 14 years older. As a result, he was cosseted and spoilt by a largely female household. Inevitably, the fact that he was so much younger than his siblings meant that he was alone at times. But he found it very easy to make friends with other children and derived enormous pleasure from reading and playing with the family pets.

Early schooling

At the age of ten, Dickie was sent to Locker's Park, a preparatory boarding school in Hertfordshire; and just under three years later, in the spring of 1913, he entered the Royal Naval College at Osborne as a cadet. He had decided to join the Royal Navy like his adored father, who was now First Sea Lord. For the first time, Dickie was known as Prince Louis, a mark of his identification with his father. Academically, he had not shone at Locker's Park; neither did he distinguish himself at Osborne. He was bullied there, but although he wrote complaining letters to his mother, he was not harmed by the experience. Slowly, he toughened up, and he dealt with his problems cheerfully.

This was partly because time away from school was idyllic. He spent long holidays abroad with his European royal relatives, being entertained in lavish style.

It was about this time – at the tender age of 13 – that Dickie fell in love for the first time. The object of his affections was his Russian cousin, the Grand Duchess Marie, daughter of Tsar Nicholas II and herself only 14. 'I was crackers about Marie, and was determined to marry her,' he wrote later. Tragically, the Romanovs were massacred a few years later.

By gracious permission of HM the Queen

Hulton-Deutsch Collection

Dickie's idyllic times came to an end in 1914 when the Great War began. Like all the young cadets, Dickie was enthusiastically excited about it, little realizing what a tragedy it would be — both internationally, and for his own family. Anti-German feeling, always present, now ran high. Even before the war, Dickie had found himself with almost no friends at Osborne because of his German background. His father spoke with a pronounced German accent all his life, and had always maintained friendly contact with his German relatives. Now, at the start of the war, things were going badly for the Royal Navy, and a scapegoat was sought. The finger was pointed at the loyal, brilliant Prince Louis, then First Sea Lord — and he was called a German spy. Although he received the support of the Navy, he felt honour-bound to resign — a cruel blow from which he never recovered.

Dickie's mother was quite typically courageous. 'We are not going to mope or hang our heads,' she said. But her husband was deeply desolate and bitter. Dickie was given the news at college. Later, as he stood to attention on the parade ground, the tears poured down his face. From that time, almost subconsciously, he was suffused with ambition.

Family honour retrieved

Over the next few years Dickie watched his hero father deteriorate, and his subsequent career can be seen as a vindication of his family's honour. He progressed from being an undistinguished pupil, and within a few years — spent at the Royal Naval College Dartmouth, and the Naval College at Keyham — he was top at every examination and his success seemed assured, as was later confirmed.

In 1917, in a bid to halt speculation about the Britishness of the Royal Family, George V proclaimed that all their Germanic names should be anglicized. The name of Saxe-Coburg-Gotha given to the Royal House by Prince Albert disappeared, to become Windsor. The Battenbergs literally translated their German name into English and became Mountbatten; they also lost royal status. It was a further cruel blow to Dickie's father.

Dickie was now officially Lord Louis Mountbatten and his parents, the First Marquis and Marchioness of Milford Haven.

A naval career

When the war ended in November 1918 Dickie was appointed second-in-command of an anti-submarine vessel, HMS *P31*. He was earning five shillings a day, and had an income of £300 a year from his father. It was acceptable, but modest — and he had no prospects. The war that had decimated his European royal relatives had also wiped out any fortune his family possessed.

In 1919, he went up to Cambridge to take a course offered to young veterans. He was starting to reap the benefits of spectacular good looks and charm. He was constantly falling in and out of love — and all the girls were simply mad about him. He was bright, witty, quick-tongued and confident — and eligible.

His one really serious attachment during these days was to Audrey James, a beautiful young debutante he fell in love with after seeing her picture in the *Tatler*. They were engaged within two weeks of meeting. But in 1920, his cousin David, the Prince of Wales, invited Dickie to accompany him as an

♔ Above *Edwina, aged one, with her mother Maud Ashley at Blackpool.* Below *Edwina in 1911, the year of her mother's death*

BROOK HOUSE

Brook House *above* – later to be the Mountbattens' home – was originally acquired by Edwina's grandfather, the wealthy banker Ernest Cassel *right* in 1906. Cassel saw the huge mansion in Park Lane as an ideal location for entertaining his influential friends, and no expense was spared in refurbishing it to this end. Eight hundred tons of Italian marble were used for the main hall and staircase and most of the rooms – including the six lavish kitchens.

In 1919, Brook House was to provide a temporary refuge for Edwina from unhappy times at home with her stepmother. When her beloved grandfather died the following year, it was left to her, and she and Dickie spent many happy years there. In 1936, however, the cost of upkeep of the house – £20,000 a year – was deemed over-extravagant and it was pulled down, to be replaced by a block of luxury apartments, although Edwina retained the top two floors as a penthouse flat

♛ *Mountbatten's trip to Australia with the Prince of Wales in 1920 marked the beginning of what was to become a close friendship. The two young men are shown* above *relaxing in a canvas bath on board* HMS Renown. *Meanwhile, Edwina numbered a high proportion of London's most eligible young men among her acquaintances. She is pictured* below *at a pheasant shoot with David's brother, Bertie, the future King of England*

aide on his tour of New Zealand, Australia and the West Indies. David did not approve of Audrey, and, like Mountbatten's family, believed that marriage to her would be a mistake. They need not have worried. Once out of range of the Mountbatten charm and good looks, Audrey had time to consider coldly what it would be like to be married to an impecunious junior naval officer, and she decided to break it off.

Dickie was shattered. But his reassuring mother consoled him with the advice that real love was qualitatively different. It was 'one of heart and head together for a girl you want to make your wife'.

The girl who was to make him thankful that Audrey turned him down was Edwina Ashley, the granddaughter of Sir Ernest Cassel. Cassel – a German-born Jew – was one of the richest men in the world, an international banker and friend of King Edward VII.

Cassel's wife had died young in 1880. They had one daughter, Maud, who married Wilfred Ashley, later to be a Conservative MP and Baron Mount Temple. This marriage produced two daughters, Edwina Cynthia Annette, born on 27 November 1901, and her sister Mary, who was five years younger.

Edwina's mother, too, died young. Edwina was only ten years old when it happened, and it marked a crescendo of misery in a childhood that had never been particularly satisfactory.

An unhappy childhood

Edwina was brought up at Broadlands, her family's estate in Hampshire. It was a beautiful 18th-century house, gracious and pleasing, with grounds designed by Capability Brown, but as a child Edwina was not happy there. With no one to restrain her – a mother who was too ill and a father who was too busy – she grew into a girl who was wilful and hard to handle. After her mother's death, things became worse.

Her father remarried and his new wife, Muriel, was the classic fairytale stepmother. Mountbatten later recalled that she was 'a wicked woman, a real bitch'. Taking over the mothering of an adolescent is not easy at the best of times, and Muriel did not feel it necessary to endear herself to her new husband's children.

Such was the two sisters' unhappiness that when it was suggested that they might go away to school, they accepted with relief, and in 1916 they were packed off to The Links, a very exclusive boarding school in Eastbourne.

Although Edwina at first enjoyed her times there, she soon began to experience difficulties with the other girls – to whom Edwina's Jewish ancestry and impending wealth became the butt of merciless taunting. 'It was sheer hell,' Edwina recalled later. 'They all thought I ought to fill the offertory plate with sovereigns on Sundays. But if I gave too much they thought I was showing off and if I gave the ordinary amount they said I was being mean.'

The one bright spot in Edwina's life was her grandfather. He was the only member of her family to have offered her unconditional affection, and now, in these troubled years, she wrote to him with increasing frequency – and desperation. 'Please take me away, dear Grandpapa, if you love me at all.' Moved, as always, by her pleas, the old man removed Edwina and her sister from The Links within two years.

Coming out in style

Her return to Broadlands, in 1918, was greeted with icy disapproval from her stepmother, and she was soon sent away again – this time to Alde House, a type of finishing school in Aldeburgh, Suffolk. After a year there, it was agreed that she would go and live with her grandfather – a plan that suited everyone.

Edwina was in her element despite the fact that her main residence was now Cassel's London home, Brook House – a huge mansion in Park Lane with an interior almost exclusively decorated with 800 tons of dark Tuscany marble; a gloomy, echoing place known (behind Cassel's back) as the 'great lavatory'. Nevertheless, Cassel was famous for his sumptuous entertaining, and Edwina soon took over all the organizing of his parties.

At 18, Edwina also 'came out' as a debutante, striking in a plain gold sheath of a dress. She was soon the talk of the town. Not only was she marked out as a considerable heiress, but she was beautiful too, willowy and slender, vivacious and intelligent. Life was one long, dazzling round of pleasure: balls and dances in town, visits to grand country houses in the company of other rich and aristocratic people. It was the perfect antidote to life at Broadlands.

Inevitably, Edwina and Dickie met at a ball. It was given by Grace Vanderbilt at Claridges in June 1921. Dickie was in the process of forgetting Audrey James, Edwina was being wooed by the Duke of Sutherland. But from the moment this attractive couple started to dance and talk they fell in love. Physically, Edwina was as stunning as Audrey James, but more unusual-looking and, as Dickie wrote shortly after the fateful meeting, 'about ten times more lively and intelligent'.

Edwina found Dickie an immensely attractive man, but also more mature than most of the young men she knew. He had been in the Navy and to university and had travelled widely. At 21, he was only a year older than she was but it seemed more. Within a few weeks, their romance was established. Everyone vied to invite them to parties together – they could not be in the same room without it being glaringly obvious to the most insensitive observer that they were madly in love. The Vanderbilts had invited Dickie along for a ten-day cruise on their yacht – now they asked Edwina aboard, too, as a last-minute guest. Shortly afterwards, he introduced her to his parents. 'My father fell head over heels for her. He said, "Edwina is the most charming and remarkable girl of this generation I have met. She's got intelligence, character, everything. If you decide to marry her you have my whole-hearted approval."'

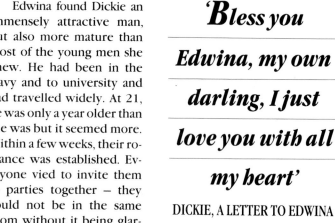

> ## 'Bless you Edwina, my own darling, I just love you with all my heart'
>
> DICKIE, A LETTER TO EDWINA

⚜ *One of the women Dickie fell most passionately in love with was a pretty debutante called Audrey James* below, *to whom he was engaged for a few weeks. She broke off the engagement on his return from Sydney. His charm and good looks ensured that he never was lonely for long – he was highly popular with all women. He is shown* bottom *being visited by a group of adoring female friends who boarded the* Renown *in Sydney to bid him farewell*

MISS AUDREY JAMES

Dickie's mother also approved – this was a real tribute, as bankers like Cassel were a class of people she normally despised.

The heiress

By September 1921, Dickie was all set to propose. He and Edwina were at Dunrobin Castle as guests of the Duke and Duchess of Sutherland, along with the Prince of Wales (by now a close friend) and the Archbishop of Canterbury among others. But that Sunday, a telegram arrived, informing Dickie that his father had died. For the moment, all thoughts of proposing were driven from his mind. The Prince of Wales, while consoling him, told him wryly, 'How lucky you are to have had such a marvellous father! If I heard my father had died, I wouldn't be able to conceal my delight.'

Then, ten days later, news came that seemed to put paid to his proposing for ever. Edwina's grandfather died.

Dickie read about it in the newspaper only days after his father's funeral. 'There it was in cold print. Death of a multi-millionaire. Edwina Ashley, great beauty of the year, now richest heiress. Over seven million pounds. Result: the question I was going to pop that very day, I didn't pop. Marriage now was out of the question.'

Money had never been an issue for Edwina, who had never had to think about it. She had no idea how much she stood to inherit because it did not seem to matter.

But Dickie's mother felt it was important. 'She said, "It never really works when the woman has so much more money than the man." From being all for the marriage, she turned against it.' Dickie was somewhat surprised at her reaction.

There seemed nothing to do but accept the Prince of Wales's invitation to join him on a tour of India and Japan. But the thought of leaving Edwina was intolerable to him. On the night before leaving London, he wrote to her, ending his letter with the tender phrases, 'Bless you Edwina, my own darling, I just love you with all my heart. Your very own Dickie.'

Before leaving Edwina, Dickie must have agonized over whether a long separation would affect her feelings as it once had done Audrey's. Forlornly he had issued a casual invitation. 'You must come out and join me – cheer things up'.

He did not really expect her to take him up on it. But then he hardly knew Edwina.

By 1921, Dickie and Edwina were already in love. When he left for India in October, Dickie was afraid he might lose her. Within months his fears would be allayed

The Mountbatten – Ashley Line

Q. Victoria m. Albert, P. of Saxe-Coburg and Gotha
(1819-1901)   (1819-1861)

Jacob Cassel   Amalia

Wilhelmina   Sir Ernest Cassel   m.   Annette Maxwell
(1852-1921)

Ps. Victoria m. P. Louis Battenberg
(1863-1950)   (1854-1921)

Maud Cassel m. Wilfrid William Ashley
(1879-1911)   Lord Mount Temple
(1867-1939)

Alice m. P. Andrew   Louise   George (2nd M.   Lord Louis m. Hon. Edwina   Mary Ashley
(1885-1969) of Hellenes (1889-1965) of Milford Haven)   Mountbatten   Ashley   (1906-1986)
(1882-1944)   (1892-1938)   (1900-1979)   (1901-1960)

P. Philip Mountbatten m. Ps. Elizabeth   Lady Patricia m. Lord Brabourne   Lady Pamela m. David Hicks
(1921-)   (1926-)   Mountbatten   (1924-)   Mountbatten   (1929-)
(1924-)   (1929-)

Edwina 1910.

♛ *Edwina with her Shetland pony,
Rusty, near Newmarket, 1910*

♛ Left *Edwina at the age of 13*

♛ *Edwina left and her sister Mary at
Broadlands, 1910*

♛ *Edwina standing, left, aged 16, with
the 1st Tennis Team at The Links*

By gracious permission of HM the Queen

♛ **Dickie** standing, right *with his* *family, 1922. Edwina is seated* far left

Syndication International

♛ *Dickie, aged six, with brother George,* *and their father, Prince Louis*

Camera Press

♛ **Dickie** right *and his brother George,* *aged 13 and 21 respectively*

Topham Picture Library

♛ *Mountbatten, aged 20, participates* *in the 'Crossing the Line' ceremony* *aboard the* Renown

Syndication International

♛ *Dickie, a proud naval* *cadet, aged 13*

Tiara-shaped head dress

⚜ The elegantly simple wedding dress in subtly gleaming silver tissue is cut on narrow lines with hanging panels and long, fitted sleeves

Bouquet of lilies with ribbon streamers

Tight sleeves cut in points over hands

Crystal and diamanté embroidery on panels

⚜ The couple in casual tweeds on their honeymoon – her skirt is a modest mid-calf length – the true 'twenties look is not apparent

⚜ To balance the basically narrow silhouette, hats were often wide brimmed to frame the face

15th century lace used for four yard-long train

THE PERFECT MATCH

Edwina Mountbatten's clothes mirrored the fashions of the day, whether frenetic 'twenties flapper or 'thirties vamp. Slim and good-looking, with the funds to indulge her taste, she became one of the best-dressed women in London. World War 2 curtailed Edwina's glamorous life style – her furs and jewels were often exchanged for the sober uniform of the St John Ambulance Brigade

Deep-crowned, deep-brimmed hat with ribbon trimming

Envelope handbag and long rope of beads

♛ The true 'flapper' style of 1927, a startling revolution in its day, brought new freedom to its wearers. Edwina's sleeveless summer dress is a typical example

♛ Edwina's elegant 'twenties wardrobe included furs for all occasions. This plush, shawl-collared beaver jacket is designed for daytime wear

Deep turned back cuffs

Flesh coloured silk stockings

♛ The 'flapper' look was completed with a head-hugging cloche hat that demanded a short hairstyle

Head-hugging hat, off the brow

Deep-crowned narrow-brimmed cloche over short hair

Silver fox fur slung around shoulders

hipped-in waist, flaring out to Princess line skirt

♛ By 1928 skirts were knee length, pleated for extra movement, as in this sharply tailored double-breasted suit

Three knife pleats

Below-knee length

♛ Typical of the 1930s, this coat i cut on asymmetric lines, with fur trimming. The waist has returned t a normal position and lengths are below the knee again

Classic court shoes

♛ Travelling smartly to India in 1947, Edwina wears a red fox fur over her checked suit. Dickie sports a double-breasted camel overcoat

Decorations pinned to wide shoulder straps

Bracelet worn over long gloves

Graduated lines of silver beading from a central point

♛ Effortlessly chic in full evening regalia – the dress is a slinky column of white crêpe, with the beading that was in vogue in 1937

♛ Two-tone shoes with a 'Louis' heel

'Louis' heels wider at base

Single or double straps with button fastening

♛ Strappy shoes – another popular 'twenties style

Hulton-Deutsch Collection

ILN Picture Library

MY ONE TRUE LOVE

BY THE TIME EDWINA JOINED DICKIE IN INDIA, HE WAS DETERMINED TO PROPOSE. THE OPULENCE OF THE WEDDING AND THE GLAMOUR OF THE HONEYMOON WERE A FORETASTE OF LIFE AHEAD

Press Association

T HE PRINCE OF WALES INVITED DICKIE TO join him on the second Empire tour as his aide. This would help him take his mind off his father's death. Although Dickie was dismayed that it would take him away from Edwina for eight months, he was thrilled by the itinerary that included India, Burma, Ceylon, Malaya and Japan, and the fact that he would meet heads of state and key politicians in each country.

Dickie loved India instantly and felt an affinity with it that was to be of major importance in the years to come. It was here, too, that he learnt to play polo – an enthusiasm he passed on successfully to his nephew, Prince Philip, and grand-nephew, Prince Charles.

But, throughout the tour, Edwina was on his mind. He would have loved to share the experiences with her, and he wrote to her often. She replied with witty, astringent letters about the 'smart set' back home. The great disparity in their wealth came to seem less and less important as the bond they felt became strengthened, rather than weakened, by his absence.

Edwina took him at his word and decided to join him in India. But there were problems: it was ironic, but the richest heiress in London was flat broke. Although Edwina's grandfather had only just died, she was not to inherit immediately; she had to be 21 before the fortune was hers, and she was still nearly a year off the magic age. Like Dickie, Edwina had been living on an allowance of £300 a year – hardly enough for a trip to India.

She had to borrow. Her great-aunt agreed to lend her £100 as long as the trip was legitimate, so Edwina managed to get an invitation from the Viceroy to stay at his residence. She had just enough for a one-way ticket to India, although it meant travelling in the most basic conditions.

Before sailing from Southampton, Edwina's doubts were only about the strength of Dickie's feelings for her, not the journey that lay ahead. She confided her fears to Dickie's brother, George, who had come to see her off. 'He absolutely worships you,' George assured her. 'Everything will be all right, you'll see.'

It was the first time Edwina had ever been outside Europe and the adventure intoxicated her. For the rest of her life, she would never mind travelling rough, indeed, she would often do so

♛ *Fate had decreed that Dickie should propose to Edwina when she joined him in India* left – *a country that would always hold a special place in both their hearts. Dickie had joined the Prince of Wales on his second tour of the Empire in late 1921.* Above *The happy times on board the* Renown *helped take his mind off his father's recent death. But he missed Edwina dreadfully and wrote to her – half seriously – to join him. She took up his offer and, overcoming all hurdles in her inimitable manner, arrived in India early the next year. They were engaged almost immediately. Edwina returned to England to prepare for the wedding, while Dickie continued with the Royal party to Japan* right. *Here, he gained insights that were to prove invaluable later*

Press Association

Popperfoto

even though she had the means to pay for the most luxurious accommodation.

When she reached Bombay, she had just enough left over for a third-class rail ticket, but although she was keen to travel packed in with Indians and their animals, it was considered unsuitable, and the Viceroy made other arrangements for her.

Edwina arrived in Delhi in February to find Dickie and the Prince of Wales's entourage working and playing hard. During the day, she was left to her own devices while the Royal party carried out a strictly timed schedule of official duties. But the evenings were an endless round of glittering parties and balls, and Edwina was included in them all.

The engagement

They had little time alone together. The Prince of Wales had a bungalow in the grounds of the Viceroy's residence, and he gave them the key, so they could snatch a moment or two alone.

Dickie knew he loved Edwina when they were in their home setting of upper-class English social life, but now he saw her in new surroundings, and was dazzled again by her. She effortlessly blended with the new setting. 'Everybody loved her,' Dickie recalled – and no one more so than the Prince of Wales, who thought she was a perfect complement to his best friend. 'David was flat out for us to get married, so, out of courtesy he telegraphed the King for his permission and I told my mother that I intended, after all, to pop the question.'

Dickie proposed, appropriately enough, at a dance held on St Valentine's Day in 1922 at the Viceregal lodge.

He noted the occasion in his diary: 'After dinner there was a small dance. I danced one and two with Edwina. She had three and four with David and the fifth dance we sat out in her sitting room, when I asked her if she would marry me, and she said she would.'

It was the perfect piece of news for a St Valentine's Day ball. Someone filled a huge punchbowl with champagne, and 17 of their friends toasted their engagement from it. It was still half full when they demanded that Dickie drain the rest. He did so – and woke up with a monumental hangover the next day. 'I felt very ill all today,' he noted weakly, 'and it is the last time I shall do anything of the sort.'

But it was his mother's consent that really mattered to Dickie. He was rewarded with a favourable reply, 'I am really and truly happy at it as I think you both know your own minds now,' his mother wrote. 'May much happiness be in store for you.'

She 'clicked' almost immediately with Edwina as they were fundamentally alike. But her mistake was to assume that Edwina would,

National Portrait Gallery

Weidenfeld Archives

Weidenfeld & Nicolson Ltd

👑 **The wedding of two of the 'brightest young things', the world's richest heiress and the young aristocrat, caught the imagination of glamour-starved, post-war Britain**

Topham Picture Library

A GLITTERING OCCASION

It was a truly Royal wedding. The Prince of Wales was best man and the bridesmaids included four princesses of Greece *left*. Dickie and Edwina were married in fashionable St Margaret's, Westminster, on 18 June 1922 by the Rector, Canon Carnegie *below left*. Among the many Royal guests inside were the King and Queen, while crowds thronged outside to see the happy couple emerge *below* – the groom resplendent in full-dress lieutenant's uniform, the bride shimmering in silver – and head for the limousine that would be towed by naval ratings

ILN Picture Library

therefore, be as happy as she was in a supporting role to a naval husband. No one, least of all Edwina, had realized that this was not to be enough for an unusual young woman who had too much energy and verve to be happy as merely a dutiful wife.

Edwina sailed for England a week after the ball. 'In London, our engagement was announced on the posters in red type four feet high side by side with the Armstrong murder case,' she wrote to Dickie. 'Isn't it swell?'

Dickie continued with the Royal tour to Ceylon, Singapore, Hong Kong and, finally, Japan. Here, he found it more difficult to negotiate the purchase of a kimono than to visit their most powerful battleship, the *Mutsu*. 'Perhaps they thought I was too young and silly to matter,' he said later, 'but, in fact, I compiled a most secret report for the Admiralty on her armour and underwater armament.'

Society wedding

The wedding of Lord Louis Mountbatten to Edwina Ashley on 18 July 1922 at St Margaret's, Westminster was a very Royal affair. The Prince of Wales was best man, and most of the organizing was done by his brother Bertie, the Duke of York. King George V invested Dickie with the order of the KCVO (Knight Commander of the Royal Victorian Order) in honour of the occasion, and, with Queen Mary, Queen Alexandra, and the Dowager Tsarina of Russia, attended the ceremony – indeed, there were representatives from the Royal Houses of Windsor, Hesse, Denmark, Saxe-Coburg-Gotha, Teck and Greece among the 1400 guests.

The bridesmaids, who wore dresses of delphinium blue, were the Princesses Margarita, Theodora, Cecile and Sophie, daughters of Mountbatten's elder sister, Princess Alice of Greece. They were accompanied to London for the wedding by their one-year-old baby brother, Prince Philip. He was too young to attend the wedding or reception, but, one day, he would feature strongly in his uncle's life – and in the British monarchy.

A crowd that reached 8000 started collecting outside the church in the early hours of the morning. Edwina wore a very 'twenties dropped-waist wedding gown, with exceedingly high heels; Dickie was in full dress uniform.

After the ceremony, the bride and groom were pulled in their car by a naval gun crew to the reception in Brook House. The wedding cake had a nautical theme, with lifebuoys and lifeboats. Among the deluge of presents, their favourite was from the Prince of Wales. He gave them a silver globe engraved with the routes of the two Royal tours that Dickie had accompanied him on. But best of all was Edwina's wedding present to Dickie – a Silver Ghost Rolls Royce.

Honeymoon de Luxe

After the reception, Dickie and Edwina set out for Broadlands, Edwina's family home, with Dickie at the wheel of the Rolls Royce. On the way down, they stopped to refuel at a garage and met a friend of Dickie's. 'D'you know my fiancée, Miss Ashley?' said Dickie, tired and befuddled from his exciting, exhausting day. It was an anecdote he often told against himself. 'I saw Edwina holding up her hand with the wedding ring, and with a resigned expression on her face. But I was still so stunned I didn't realize it.'

They stayed a few days at Broadlands, not emerging till lunchtime each day, and only leaving the grounds once on a trip to Southampton to see a newsreel film of their wedding. Then the real holiday began.

They had decided to start their marriage in the most hedonistic way possible – with a honeymoon six months long. Dickie had to apply for leave on half-pay, but he deduced rightly that never again would this be granted him with no protest.

This was the first time that the young couple had serious money to play with. On her marriage, even though she was not yet 21, Edwina had inherited all her wealth. Previously, as befitted an unmarried girl, the only jewellery she had been allowed had been a pearl necklace. Now she packed a trunkload of jewels and designer clothes.

They sailed for France to motor through to Spain and Germany. With military precision, Dickie had devised a touring schedule of Europe as organized and foolproof as a royal tour. This did not suit Edwina, whose idea of fun and excitement meant branching out into the unknown and uncharted. Dickie reluctantly threw away his plans. The result of this was that, although they stayed at the Ritz in Paris, they spent the first night out of Paris in a single bed in an attic room – bliss for Edwina.

But after that, it was a palace-hopping round of royal relatives. First was Spain to visit Dickie's cousin, Queen Ena, and her husband King Alfonso. They watched a bull-fight, and the King presented Dickie with the Grand Cross of Isabella the Catholic.

Next, they visited Uncle Ernie, the Grand Duke of Hesse, in Germany. This was Dickie's opportunity to introduce Edwina to his German heritage. To his great pleasure, Edwina loved meeting his family and getting to know about his background. However, the

♔ *Edwina and Dickie embarked on their married life in the manner they meant to continue – with verve and style. After Paris, they motored in the Rolls to Spain and Germany. But the honeymoon had hardly begun, and soon they embarked on a tour of the United States*

THE MOUNTBATTENS IN HOLLYWOOD

It was only natural that a couple leading such enchanted lives should visit the home of 20th-century fantasy – Hollywood. As befitted their 'star' status, they stayed at the home of celluloid royalty, Douglas Fairbank's and Mary Pickford's famous house, Pickfair. Here, Charlie Chaplin produced a movie for them, *Nice and Friendly*, which featured Jackie

Coogan, the Mountbattens and their valet. And although Chaplin had to console a downcast Dickie whose performance left much to be desired, it did not dampen Dickie's inexhaustible enthusiasm. He continued to take a very active interest in filming, introduced it to the Royal Navy and, later, founded the Royal Naval Film Corporation

The Bodley Head/Weidenfeld Archives

Syndication International

The Bodley Head/Weidenfeld Archives

visit did not go down too well in certain quarters back home. The *Daily Mail* bristled, 'that the Mountbattens should choose to stay in Germany, for their honeymoon, is surely a *faux pas*'. But the visit had its advantages – raging inflation in post-war Germany meant that Dickie was able to buy his sister Louise a fur stole for just over £2.

The newspapers charted their progress through Europe by Rolls Royce, luxury liners and first-class trains. Inevitably, there was some criticism, but on the whole, their antics were followed with pleasure by the readers. They epitomized the fantasies of the masses caught up in post-war gloom, a Hollywood dream of a honeymoon. As an onlooker of the time said: 'They were quite simply the most glamorous and sought-after people in society. Everyone loved them.'

The love affair with America

In the autumn, the couple sailed for the United States, occupying a sumptuous suite in the luxury liner, the *Majestic*. Their reception as they docked in New York startled even Dickie, who found himself invited to meet the President in Washington and to address a battery of admirals and senior officers at a dinner. They were lionized by the press and famous personalities, who, in true democratic fashion, were fascinated by Dickie's royal connections and Edwina's millions.

The atmosphere of New York suited Edwina's temperament exactly. 'I loved its sharpness and liveliness,' she remembered afterwards. 'Everybody was awake and alert, and ready for something new.' She could have been describing her own personality. From the East Coast, they made their luxurious way across in a private coach by rail to Niagara Falls and Chicago, Salt Lake City and then California.

The couple, who might have stepped out of a Hollywood film, soon found themselves in one. In Hollywood, they borrowed the home of Douglas Fairbanks and Mary Pickford, an elegant mansion called Pickfair. There, they were joined by Charlie Chaplin and Jackie Coogan. Chaplin and the Mountbattens hit it off immediately. They were to remain life-long friends and Dickie was instrumental in having him honoured with a knighthood many years later. Edwina, especially, found Chaplin extremely compatible, given his quick-wittedness, sense of fun and Jewish background.

Knowing Dickie's fascination with films, they decided to make one themselves – a short, silent (and, of course, funny) film called *Nice and Friendly* in which they played, appropriately enough, a pair of young lovers. Chaplin directed and gave it to them as a wedding present. But it was a miracle it ever got made, as

UPI/Bettmann Newsphotos

♛ *America loved the Mountbattens, and they, in turn, fell in love with America. It had youth, originality, wealth and exuberance – qualities they prized and epitomized. From the minute they landed, they were fêted by leading personalities, from the President in Washington, to show-biz and sports luminaries in New York, such as 'Babe' Ruth, the legendary baseball player* left

they spent most of the time dissolved in giggles.

Dickie, never one to let an opportunity pass, also took the time to extend his knowledge of the technical side of film-making. He spent hours with the famous director, Cecil B de Mille, asking detailed questions.

After Hollywood, the rest of the trip was a kaleidoscopic blur of sightseeing. They visited the Grand Canyon and Florida, always treated like royalty, always entertained by the top people, and finally ended up in New York ready for the trip home.

Home at last

The wonderful honeymoon ended just before Christmas. They disembarked from the luxury liner that had brought them from New York at Southampton on 23 December 1922, so loaded with presents and acquisitions that they had to leave most of their trunks behind. Dickie's brother, George, met them at the port and took them

off to spend Christmas with himself and his family – an essential wind-down before real life started.

It was a glamorous start to a marriage that should have been perfect. But both of them were too blinded by love to recognize that there were fundamental problems that would rock their marriage almost as soon as it started. They loved each other's essential strength and character, but were not going to have an easy ride.

During a press conference in New York, they were asked how they saw their marriage. 'Career for Lady Louis?' Mountbatten had answered blithely, 'Why she's going to be my wife, that's career enough.' And, the press had wanted to know of Edwina, 'What do you think about the conduct of the modern woman and divorce, ma'am?' Edwina had answered demurely, 'Oh, I just believe in being an old-fashioned wife.' The trouble was, Edwina was joking and Dickie was not.

♛ *The Mountbattens' three-month tour took them from New York via Niagara Falls and Chicago to Los Angeles and Hollywood, and back through the Grand Canyon – which Dickie noted, with more precision than imagination, as 'an average 13 miles wide, 1 mile deep and 200 miles long'. Then, on to Florida and back to New York to wave goodbye to an adoring American public and embark for home, just in time for Christmas with the family*

General View, Niagara Falls.

THE BILTMORE HOTEL
LOS ANGELES

FOUNTAIN IN EOLA PARK, ORLANDO, FLORIDA—78

Popperfoto

BROADLANDS

The family home of Edwina Mountbatten is situated on a curve of the River Test near the Hampshire market town of Romsey. Originally part of a Norman abbey, Broadlands was bought in 1736 by Edwina's ancestor, the first Lord Palmerston, and redesigned by his grandson and heir, Henry Temple. Broadlands today is a tribute to his exemplary good taste – a rare mixture of grandeur and domesticity

Jeremy Whitaker

♛ The antique busts show to good effect in the octagonal, skylit Domed Hall *top*, which offers a tantalizing glimpse of the Sculpture Hall beyond

♛ The Sculpture Hall *above* provides a suitably architectural setting for the statuary bought by the second Lord Palmerston on his numerous 'Grand Tours' of Europe

♛ The Dining Room *right* was designed by Henry Holland in 1788. The three full-length portraits, bought by Edwina's grandfather, are by Van Dyck

Jeremy Whitaker

Photographers International

👑 The stunning plasterwork of the Saloon *above* was completed by Joseph Rose the elder in 1769. The arched recesses at either end of the room originally contained statues of the goddesses Ceres and Hygeia, which are now on display in the entrance hall. Mountbatten family photographs *left* add an intimate touch to the neo-Classical decoration

Photographers International

Jeremy Whitaker

♔ The Portico Room *below,* with its glorious views of the River Test, makes the perfect honeymoon suite. The borders around the wall panels pick up the floral design of the chintz bedhangings

♔ The Green Room *above* takes its name from the colour scheme and its prospect of countryside from the windows. The portrait of Edwina on the wall by the bed was painted by PA de Laszlo in 1924

♔ The Wedgwood Room *above* contains a priceless collection of Josiah Wedgwood's pottery. The elaborate mouldings and friezes, fitted bookcases and arched mirror form an exquisite whole

♔ The Ionic portico of the Orangery *below* gives it the air of a temple amid the tranquillity of Capability Brown's landscape. The gardens of Broadlands are among Brown's finest achievements

Rex Features

Jeremy Whitaker

FAMILY AFFAIRS

ON THE SURFACE, MARRIED LIFE WAS A PERPETUAL PARTY, BUT A YOUNG FAMILY DEMANDED RESPONSIBILITY. EDWINA'S RESTLESS SPIRIT AND DICKIE'S RELENTLESS AMBITION WERE ON A COLLISION COURSE

IT TOOK A LITTLE ADJUSTMENT BEFORE Mountbatten could settle back into naval life after the excitement of the honeymoon. He could take the physical hardships, but the coldness he encountered from his fellow sailors was harder to handle. The problem was that he and his rich wife were now celebrities. He had to battle against the fact that what people were able to glean about him was all superficial – the glamour side, which made him sound an idle, empty-headed aristocratic oaf with more money than was good for him. As he remembered wryly, 'Every time I joined a new ship, I had to start absolutely afresh. I would probably arrive in the wardroom at the same time as a copy of the latest *Tatler* with pictures of me on leave. You could see absolutely the suspicion and hostility which I then had to break down.' The only way to gain the respect of his shipmates was to work hard, and offer to take on disagreeable chores to show that he was 'one of the boys'.

The first child

Certainly, off-duty life was as glamorous as ever. Edwina overhauled the gloomy Brook House, diluting the effect of its dark marble with new curtains and carpets. They regularly gave huge dinner parties for a hundred guests at a time, and it was common for the guests to work off the effects of the meal in the mansion's own Turkish baths afterwards. Later, they bought Adsdean, a house in Portsmouth, useful because Mountbatten had to spend a lot of time there. In both they entertained lavishly, with a guest list that mixed film stars with royalty and key decision-makers in politics and the services.

But they had their cosy moments too – times that epitomized what Dickie most wanted from married life. 'Dined alone with Edwina, and read aloud as usual afterwards,' was a common entry in his diary. But although

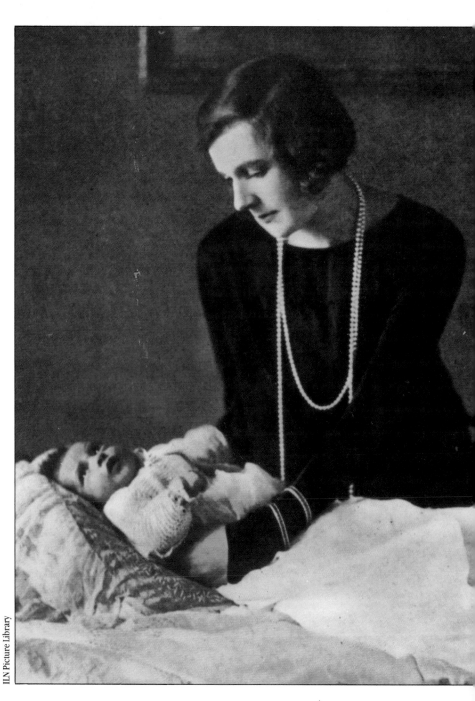

this way of spending an evening was a delight to him, it was something that quickly bored and irritated Edwina.

Mountbatten's energy was extraordinary. One of the annoying things to those at the same level was that, despite the fact that he burned the candle at both ends, his career flourished outstandingly. He had chosen to specialize in signals because it was an area of communications which fascinated him, and in 1924 he took a signals course at Portsmouth and characteristically finished it top of his class.

As important to him as this, however, was that his baby daughter Patricia was born on St Valentine's Day that year. Dickie was in Madeira at the time, and was beside himself with excitement when the news reached him. 'My dear, dear darling little mother,' he wrote to Edwina. 'I could hardly hold myself in when I got the wireless message this morning saying that our daughter had been born . . . I think it's just so wonderful that I feel quite *drunk* about it.'

With typical Mountbatten luck he played roulette shortly after hearing the news, placed his chips to win on nought – his baby's age – and won. The moment he was back in London and saw the baby he 'fell in love with her' and continued to adore her throughout her life.

Edwina was less excited about her new role as mother. Within a few months of the birth she left Patricia behind to go with Dickie and the Prince of Wales in a group to New York. It was summertime and the Royal guests partied throughout the trip, arriving back in London in time for a further whirl of activity.

Edwina's indiscretions

With Dickie now working so hard, Edwina became restless. It was inevitable that it would happen sooner or later, but the fact that he was so occupied precipitated her discontent. Playing housewife, mother and little wife would never have suited her at the best of times. Barbara Cartland, a close friend of the couple, said, 'Edwina was a complex personality because she had a man's brain in the body of a very beautiful woman.' A close friend commented: 'There was always something missing. She didn't know what it was or where it was, but she was determined to find it.'

The search was two-fold – travel and other men. It was only three years after the marriage, in 1925, that Dickie became aware for the first time that Edwina was unfaithful. 'I was terribly upset, and found it hard to believe,' he said many years afterwards – a reserved understatement. He had naïvely expected total fidelity from Edwina, and was fully prepared to offer it himself. But she could not be restrained, and

Hulton-Deutsch Collection

👑 **The birth of daughter Patricia** opposite *in 1924 was a joy to Mountbatten.* **But Edwina, who loathed domestic routine, continued her freewheeling life style** *above.* **Mountbatten compensated for her frequent absences by indulging his grand passion for polo** *below.* **His book,** Introduction to Polo, *written under the pseudonym of 'Marco', remains a valuable guide to the sport*

Dickie's attempts to restrict her were only half-hearted. For Dickie's life was ruled by twin passions – his love for Edwina and his drive to make his mark in his career. Another man might have felt that it was worth cutting down on his ambitions to make more time for his wife, but Dickie would continue to reserve his best energies for his work.

In 1925, Edwina took off on what was the first of her lengthy expeditions. Leaving husband and baby without a qualm, she headed for adventure. With just the occasional letter home, she travelled freely. At one point, she signed up as an ordinary member of the crew of a sailing schooner trading among the Polynesian islands. She did not return until the spring of 1926.

Back in England, she plunged enthusiastically into thwarting the strikers during the General Strike, manning the switchboard of the *Daily Express* conscientiously. Later that year, she shocked many by attending a ball at Buckingham Palace in a sensational dress made of nothing but silver sequins.

By 1927, the Mountbattens had moved to Malta, where Mountbatten had joined the Mediterranean Fleet as Assistant Wireless Officer on the battleship HMS *Warspite*. Edwina followed his ship in their smart white yacht, *The Shrimp*, giving parties aboard when at anchor. Later, they acquired a house on Malta where they continued to give parties almost every night, Edwina dreaming up wacky

> ## *'Edwina . . . had a man's brain in the body of a very beautiful woman'*
> ### BARBARA CARTLAND

ideas and themes that made invitations there the most sought-after on the island.

But being known as a brilliant hostess could never be enough for Edwina. She continued to take off on her travels regularly, often with a tiny holdall containing only shorts, shirts and one dress. She would usually go with a female companion who, like Edwina, did not mind living rough. Over the years she went to Persia, Egypt, the West Indies, Asia and all over the Far East. Once she came back with a lion cub she had bought. Both the Mountbattens adored animals, the more exotic the better. They also had a chameleon, two kangaroos, a mongoose, a bushbaby and a honey bear. The bear was once locked out of the house for a misdemeanour but it tunneled back in again, uprooting the parquet floor.

Dickie used to miss Edwina dreadfully. 'Lovely to see the old girl again,' he would note forlornly in his diary, or 'Divine having the old girl back.' But his private misery did not affect his career. In April 1928, Mountbatten was promoted to Lieutenant-Commander. He also developed his passion for polo.

Edwina's affairs continued. Round about that time, she was cited as co-respondent in a divorce case in the United States, which had to be hushed up in England.

ILN Picture Library

Popperfoto

Hulton-Deutsch Collection

Weidenfeld Archives

LORD AND LADY LOUIS MOUNTBATTEN.

LADY LOUIS MOUNTBATTEN AND "THE PEOPLE"

LIBEL ACTION SETTLED: APOLOGY IN COURT

Lady Louis Mountbatten was the plaintiff in a libel action, Mountbatten v. Odhams Press Limited and Another, before the Lord Chief Justice in the King's Bench Division on Friday.

Mr Birkett, K.C., announced that the action had been settled.

He said that Odhams Press Limited were the proprietors of "The People," the editor of which, Mr Harry Ainsworth, was also a defendant in the action.

him nor had anything whatsoever to do with him in any shape or form

"As soon as the libel appeared in print every endeavour was made to track down the originator of this foul rumour.

"Lady Louis Mountbatten was compelled to bring the proceedings publicly to vindicate her good name. If the case had been fought out in court it would have been the right of Lady Louis Mountbatten to go into the box to deal with those matters on oath.

"She desires this morning," added Mr Birkett, "to ask your lordship's permission, despite the course the defendants have taken, to go into the box to deny upon oath these poisonous allegations.

"Defendants had never sought to defend the action. Immediately complaint was made that the name of Lady Louis Mountbatten was being associated with this article they did everything in their power to mitigate the very grievous wrong which had been committed.

"The defendants had given to Lady Louis Mountbatten the fullest indemnity for the costs and expenses to which she had been put, and an unqualified apology and withdrawal which they intended to repeat again in court through Sir Patrick Hastings.

"There is one further matter of some importance," added Mr Birkett. "Your lordship will appreciate from what I have already said in this undefended case that Lady Louis Mountbatten was in a position to demand not only damages, but exceedingly heavy damages from the defendants.

Without Doubt

"Without the smallest doubt a jury would have awarded very heavy damages, and there are no limits to the sum which a jury might have awarded in this case.

"Lady Louis desired it to be made plain that in the circumstances of this case no money that could be named would be adequate to compensate her for the anguish misery and distress which this libel has caused.

"To accept one single penny would be to her in the highest degree distasteful. What she did desire was that she should have a speedy and public vindication of

ILN Picture Library

♛ *An uneasy truce developed in the Mountbatten marriage – they spent a happy few days in Monte Carlo with daughter, Patricia, in 1932 left. Edwina continued to be anxious to maintain the right public image, however, and she is shown above, all smiles, with Patricia and Pamela. In reality, she saw little of the two girls*

♛ *Edwina's name had already been linked with several men when her affair with Laddie Sandford* far left *became an open secret in the late 1920s. In 1932, Edwina successfully sued* The People *newspaper over a story linking her with the entertainer Paul Robeson* left. *But many believed there was no smoke without fire, and King George V and Queen Mary were said to be appalled by her behaviour. Following the Robeson scandal, she rarely received an invitation to court – 'I don't give a rap' was her characteristic response*

Shortly afterwards Edwina became pregnant with their second child, although this did not stop her taking off on yet another trip. This one was to Egypt to study archaeology. Heavily pregnant, she then arranged to meet Dickie in Barcelona. Typically, she made no concessions to her state, and had a hard and tiring journey to the rendezvous. The effect of this was to start her labour prematurely. From their suite at the Ritz, Dickie frantically arranged medical assistance. At one point it looked as if the baby – a second daughter who was to be called Pamela – might die, but both mother and baby were healthy and suffered no ill effects.

For a while, this panic drew the couple closer together. Edwina wrote to Dickie, 'I think it takes sometimes a crisis like this to make one realize just how much one cares for a person. I don't think there can be anything *seriously* wrong if we feel like I think we both did, during this last week.'

To Dickie's great distress they never had any more children. He was hoping for a son to continue his name and the glittering naval tradition. However, his nephew, the young Prince Philip, who arrived to be educated in England when he was eight years old, became like a son to him, and in later years it was Mountbatten

who suggested that the prince-without-a-name, take the surname Mountbatten before his marriage to the Princess Elizabeth.

As a father, Dickie was always far more involved with his children than was Edwina. They were very important to him – and he to them. Their mother was a remote, perfumed figure who would disappear for months on end without warning. He was the one who would take the time to put them to bed and read to them, invent games for them, join them for breakfast, and share with them his personal opinions and philosophy. As he once said to Patricia: 'I don't believe God will strike you dead if you lie, but people won't rely on you and in the end you won't be clever enough to remember what you said before, and you'll be caught out.'

The strain tells

Edwina was jealous – not because her children were more attached to their father, but because they were so important to him. She did not want to be wholly his, but she wanted him to be all hers.

These were the years of greatest estrangement for the Mountbattens, but the tie between them was strong. Dickie still relied heavily on Edwina's support and clear thinking. She would admonish him when he was down with the words, 'Rise above it, Dickie! Worse things happen at sea!'

But he still had to put up with her increasingly open involvement with other men. During the late 1920s, Laddie Sandford was her favourite – a rich, polo-playing American whom Dickie seemed to loathe. Despite his apparent indifference, he was deeply hurt. He wrote to

Edwina that Sandford had been 'the cause of pretty well all the unhappiness I have known'.

This may well have been a crisis point in their relationship, but he chose not to leave her and that meant that he just had to accept her the way she was. 'I offer you all my sympathetic understanding about Laddie,' he wrote, and promised that he would 'try to feel nicely about him always'.

An extraordinary love letter that Dickie wrote to Edwina in 1927 sets out his anguish and conflict, and explains his decision to put up with whatever she might do. Part of it read, 'I wish I could drive a car like Bobby Casa Maury, play the piano and talk Culture like Peter … shoot like Daddy … play polo like Jack. I wish I knew how to flirt with other women, and especially with my wife. I wish I had sown more wild oats in my youth, and could excite you more than I fear I do … In other words, I would like to feel that I was really worthy of your love … I have properly let my pen run away with my thoughts but I am different from you in that I must unbottle my feelings to someone, and in my case this could only be to you who are so much more than a mere wife and lover to me. You see, my sweet, you happen to be my first, principal and truest friend. That's why I love you so.'

A new understanding

Dickie was able to come to terms with Edwina's infidelities to such an extent that he liked her to tell him about them, and to a certain degree was proud of them, particularly when he valued the man involved.

But he remained faithful to Edwina. He always loved pretty women, and surrounded himself with them whenever he could. At one point his office was so full of attractive young women that they were called 'Dickie's harem'. His official biographer maintains that sex was not important to him and that he was happy with friendships rather than affairs. Partly because of this, and partly because he also enjoyed the company of young men, it has often been suggested that he was homosexual. But this has never been more than a rumour. Certainly, it is extremely unlikely – any scandal of that sort would have finished his career, which was more important to him than anything else.

But despite the fact that Dickie did not have affairs, and was so considerate of Edwina's, she was ragingly jealous of any close friendships he had with women. One of them, Yola Letellier, whom Mountbatten met in 1926, and who remained his best female friend throughout his life, particularly enraged her. Edwina's strategy for coping with this was to make friends with Yola herself, in a bid to nip the relationship in the bud.

THE 'SMART SET'

Edwina was 'definitely one of the leaders of the "smart set",' said Mountbatten, and he himself was amused to be considered an arbiter of fashion in the heady days of the Roaring Twenties and early 1930s. Their circle was made up of royalty, film stars and rich socialites, including *below* his special friend, Yola Letellier (second from right, next to Edwina), also *clockwise*, cousin David and Mrs Simpson, and Mary Pickford *extreme left*; Noël Coward; and Norma Shearer (with David Niven). The social season revolved around Ascot, Cowes and Goodwood. When 'in town', the rich and famous threw themselves into a dizzy whirl of parties and balls, from the Ritz to the Cafe Royal, from the Kit-Cat Club to Monsignor's (pictured *below centre* in a contemporary illustration), a restaurant and nightclub in the West End. In the small hours, a select group of guests would often be invited back to the Mountbattens' opulent penthouse, seen *below left* through the trees of Hyde Park. This boasted, among other features, the 'fastest lift in London' and its own cinema; the apartment was once the scene of a sumptuous ball for 500 revellers

ILN Picture Library

Country Life

ILN Picture Library

31

TIMES OF CHANGE

Mountbatten's naval career continued to progress steadily. In 1932 he was promoted to Commander, and in 1934 he was given his own ship. Then, two years later, he was recalled to England to take up a job in the Naval Air Division of the Admiralty, and was made responsible for the Fleet Air Arm.

He was already fully convinced that war with Germany was inevitable, so the job suited him very well. A strong air force was going to be essential, and he knew the Navy would have a vital part to play. He put forward a strong case for funds to be made available so that he could do all in his power to modernize and streamline the Fleet Air Arm. But for a while Mountbatten was frustrated as his words fell on deaf ears.

Life at the top

Things were changing at home too. Throughout the 1920s and early 1930s, Edwina had been spending an average of £20,000 a year to maintain Brook House. At last she was convinced that this was ostentatious wastage, and she bowed to pressure from her lawyers to do something about it. The solution was to pull down the marble monstrosity and put up a block of luxury flats. For sentimental reasons, she called the new building Brook House. The top two floors she kept for themselves – it was London's first penthouse, and no other has ever been so extraordinary. Soaring into the sky, it was flood-lit at night. She filled it with gadgets and decorated it in the 1930s version of high-tech. It had 30 rooms, five of which had partition walls and could be made into a ballroom or a 150-seat cinema. The private lift was Mountbatten's special joy, 'the non-stop fastest lift in London'.

This penthouse was the Mountbattens' home in London until the outbreak of war. It was a millionaire's fantasy of a place, and friends and acquaintances were constantly angling for party invitations. Guests included George Bernard Shaw and Noël Coward, and, as war drew near, Brook House was also the venue for informal meetings between Mountbatten and powerful political figures like Winston Churchill.

Abdication crisis

In 1936 King George V had died and had been succeeded by Mountbatten's best friend David – now known as King Edward VIII. Mountbatten watched in appalled fascination as it became clear that David was going to give up his throne in order to marry the divorcee Wallis Simpson. Mountbatten had never been able to understand in more than the vaguest way David's conduct of his private life. He had always been surrounded by a loving family himself, and would

Associated Press

'BERTIE' GETS A BOOST

Mountbatten had never been close to his cousin 'Bertie', pictured here arriving at Portsmouth with the Queen for the Review of the Fleet in 1937. But Mountbatten provided discreet support from the sidelines during the abdication crisis of 1936, and Bertie's accession to the throne as King George VI. The new King was convinced that he simply did not have the makings of a monarch – 'I'm only a naval officer; it's the only thing I know about,' he said. But Mountbatten was greatly impressed with him, and his answer was heartfelt: 'There is no more fitting preparation for a King than to have been trained in the navy.' Support from such a respected quarter did wonders for George VI's morale

Hulton-Deutsch Collection

Hulton-Deutsch Collection

Press Association

👑 *The Mountbattens – seen together above left in Florida in 1938 – were as old as the century and in the late 1930s their relationship reflected a new maturity. In the early months of 1939, Edwina put behind her more than a decade of carefree living when she joined the Women's Voluntary Services to do her bit for the coming war. She is pictured above centre with her friend Lady Forbes, sorting out warm garments to send to Royal Navy recruits. Mountbatten meanwhile was involved at the very highest level in the navy's war preparations*

never have invested so much importance in one other person – even in Edwina, whom he adored. David, in contrast, had had a loveless childhood and an empty life until Wallis had filled it. But Mountbatten believed in duty above everything and he found his cousin's decision incomprehensible: 'I always thought it was his duty to remain King and told him that he ought to give up Wallis.' Mountbatten believed above everything in the importance of monarchy, and his support for the new King George VI, following Edward VIII's abdication, was considerable. But he remained friends with the Windsors. 'Edwina and I were too fond of them both for there to be any breaks,' he said.

Rising star
Mountbatten's work in the Naval Air Division earned him promotion to Captain of a flotilla of destroyers in June 1937. 'Promoted at 37.0. Average age 42–5,' he recorded with typical boastfulness. Not the least of his contributions to the Royal Navy was the inauguration of the Royal Naval Film Corporation, a body set up to organize and oversee the showing of feature films for the entertainment of shipboard crews. By 1938, Mountbatten's fears about the coming war were being proved right, and he was given the go-ahead to make any

> ## *'He possesses a naïve simplicity with a compelling manner and dynamic energy'*
> MOUNTBATTEN'S NAVAL REPORT, 1938

improvements he deemed necessary to the Fleet Air Arm.

In the same year, Edwina made an expedition to the Far East with two women friends. There, she insisted on driving them all along the highly dangerous 800-mile Burma Road. This was something that previously only hardened Chinese truck drivers had attempted.

On the journey, she faced not just the natural hazards of the unyielding terrain, but possible attack by Japanese soldiers, for the Chinese had built the road as a supply line in their war against Japan. This was exactly the sort of feat that satisfied Edwina's thirst for adventure and danger, especially when she had been warned not to attempt it.

'She did so love confounding those who thought they knew best,' remarked a friend. 'The word "impossible" was sheer nectar to Edwina, just as danger was a heady scent that she could not resist.'

Finding direction
It was a quality that had never been harnessed before, but the war was about to make use of it. For the first time Edwina's talents and energies were to have real direction, and the improvement in her marriage was going to be enormous.

PEERS OF THE REALM

As a descendant of both the British and German Royal Families, Louis Mountbatten's lineage was of enviable calibre. And in the service of his country, in which he excelled, he gathered an extraordinary array of titles — the laurels of the British Honours system — which placed both him and Edwina up within the very highest echelons of British Royalty

Mansell Collection

Baron/Camera Press

THE MOUNTBATTEN CREST

Mountbatten's family crest bears the emblems of his German forbears. The lions represent the Grand Duchy of Hesse and the striped pallets on the right-hand shield signify the Battenberg line

Hulton-Deutsch Collection

ORDER OF THE GARTER

In 1946, Mountbatten was awarded the Order for his military achievements — it is limited to 24 Knights Companion. The Earl is seen attending the annual ceremony at Windsor in 1965

THE COAT OF ARMS
Mountbatten's heraldry with the House of Windsor shield *inset*

LORD AND LADY MOUNTBATTEN
The Earl and Countess in full regalia attending the Coronation of Queen Elizabeth in 1953

SERVANT OF THE EMPIRE
Lavished with awards, Mountbatten wears the Orders of Merit, the Bath, the Garter and Star of India

IN MEMORIAM
A stone dedicated to Dickie and Edwina sits in Westminster Abbey

Telegraph Colour Library

Rex Features

Hulton–Deutsch Collection

Imperial War Museum

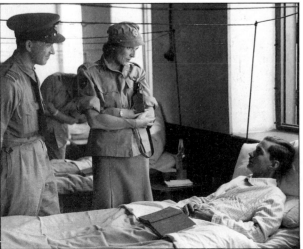

Hulton–Deutsch Collection

♛ *1941 and the sinking of HMS Kelly centre left* marked a major turning point in Mountbatten's career. The fearlessness and strong personal gifts he showed during the drama singled him out as a man of destiny.

He took over as Supreme Allied Commander of South East Asia in 1943. His achievements – in Burma *top especially* – were ultimately rewarded with Japan's unconditional surrender in 1945 *left*.

During all this time, and for long after the end of the war, Edwina *far left* worked with great dedication as a representative of the Red Cross and St John Ambulance Brigade, visiting the sick and wounded throughout the Far East

Syndication International

FOR KING AND COUNTRY

THE 1940S AND '50S WERE YEARS OF OUTSTANDING ACHIEVEMENT FOR THE MOUNTBATTENS, AND DESPITE EDWINA'S MUCH-PUBLICIZED AFFAIRS, THE COUPLE ENJOYED A NEW-FOUND CLOSENESS

AR, AS MOUNTBATTEN had predicted, finally broke out in 1939. At the time, Mountbatten was commander of the Fifth Destroyer Flotilla led by HMS *Kelly.* Although Mountbatten did not welcome war, it brought out the best in him. He was courageous and a natural leader. As captain on the *Kelly,* he was always leading his men into danger – but they adored and admired him. It was common for a wounded sailor to want to return to fight under Mountbatten once his injuries had healed. One of Mountbatten's officers said, with admiration rather than criticism, that his captain thought 'that nothing was really worth doing unless it was slightly dangerous'.

The Kelly incident

The sinking of the *Kelly* off the coast of Crete in 1941 showed the qualities in Mountbatten that inspired devotion. He was, almost inevitably, the last to leave the ship as she went down.

Dying and injured men were in the water as the aeroplanes that had bombed the *Kelly* sprayed them with machine guns to try to pick off the survivors. Mountbatten remembered that, as the planes swung away and the exhausted sailors pulled themselves on to a raft, 'the sea was beautifully warm and dead calm – just the sort of sea people look forward to when they go to the Mediterranean for a holiday. But now we all needed cheering up, so I called for a song or two. We began with "Roll out the Barrel". The *Kelly* wasn't far off, bottom up, but she was going, so I called out "Three cheers for the old ship!" And then down she went.'

♔ *The war introduced a sense of real purpose into both Dickie's and Edwina's lives. They were now a working couple sharing a common cause. As a result they promoted not merely their country, but also the happiness and fulfilment of their own marriage*

There was no one like Mountbatten for keeping up the spirits of his men, even when they were wounded and defeated. The name of *Kelly* lives on because Noël Coward based a film on her adventures. *In Which We Serve* was hugely successful, though some thought – erroneously – that Mountbatten had engineered it as a self-publicizing venture.

Edwina's war

War had a dramatic effect on Edwina. Suddenly, she had a legitimate focus for her huge energies. As one of her friends said, 'All that rushing about was finished anyway. She was like a bluebottle that is driven nearly frantic in a room and suddenly finds the open window.'

The Mountbattens packed Patricia and Pamela off to New York for safety. Mountbatten justified this by explaining, 'With their Jewish blood [from Edwina's side] they would have been the first for the gas ovens if the Germans had invaded.' Then they radically restrained their glamorous life style. They locked up their sumptuous penthouse in Brook House and moved into a small house; they also turned over Broadlands, which Edwina had now inherited, to be used as a hospital.

With home responsibilities now so streamlined, Edwina was ready for action. First, she joined the Women's Volunteer Service and then the St John Ambulance Brigade. In November 1939, she was appointed county president for London of the St John Ambulance Brigade.

Her involvement was not confined to being a name on the letterhead. She raised money, went into hospitals to see what should be done – and

then made it happen. Once the blitz began in London, she visited air-raid shelters night after night, encouraging and raising morale. 'My wife's courage was fantastic during the Blitz,' Mountbatten said later. 'She really didn't know what fear was about.'

One major consequence was that their relationship started to improve. They saw more of each other than at any other period since their marriage began, and they were working for a common cause. Edwina continued to have affairs, and to be spiky and difficult at times, but they valued each other more and more.

In 1941, they went to the United States together, a sober visit vastly different from the fun-loving sorties they had made before. Edwina's brief was to tour the country on behalf of the British Red Cross and St John Ambulance Brigade and to thank those who had contributed over five million pounds to their efforts. Dickie helped by coaching her in public speaking —

one of his fortes. He was in the United States to check on the *Illustrious*, a carrier undergoing repairs, which he was to captain on its voyage back to England.

After his heroic captaincy of the *Kelly*, Mountbatten found his prestige had increased a hundredfold. Throughout the six years of the war, he was promoted at enormous speed, and jobs were created to take advantage of his unique talents. Just 39 at the outbreak of the war, he found himself in charge of men, all much older than himself. Inevitably, some resented his meteoric rise.

At Churchill's request, he became Chief of Combined Operations, which meant that he was part of the team that planned the landings in North Africa and Sicily, and then he was made Supreme Allied Commander of South East Asia — in charge of 'the forgotten army'. The American press complained that their own General MacArthur, a man 20 years older than Mountbatten, should have been given the job, and that he had been snubbed in favour of 'a London glamour boy'. But Mountbatten's appointment was proved to be brilliantly inspired. His tactical fighting plan gave the troops a stunning success.

In early 1945, Mountbatten was told by Churchill of plans to drop the atomic bomb on Hiroshima. He immediately shared this heavy knowledge with Edwina. When attacked for having told his wife something that should have remained strictly confidential, Mountbatten replied, 'I had no secrets from Edwina.' His only regret was that she sometimes had secrets from him, or would open her heart more to her current lover than her husband.

♛ *Mountbatten's work in India was demanding and moments of relaxation with Edwina, such as that shown* below *outside the New Delhi palace, were rare. For the most part it was a time of gruelling negotiations with leaders such as Mahatma Gandi* right *which called upon all his reserves of charm and diplomacy*

In September 1945, the Japanese war ended and Mountbatten travelled to Singapore to receive the formal surrender. Edwina accompanied him in her official capacity. She was now Superintendent-in-Chief of the St John Ambulance Brigade, simply because her contribution had been superb. Like Mountbatten, she was courageous and tireless, and not afraid of mucking in, or helping out in tragic and sometimes disgusting circumstances. She only used her name and influence to gain improvements for others, particularly in ill-equipped hospitals. Mountbatten authorized her to travel to the Far East, locating prisoners-of-war and internment camps and doing what she could for the inmates. She journeyed 33,000 miles, through 16 countries, hardly resting or sleeping. The story she had to report back to her husband was grim. She had met survivors of terrifying and obscene tortures, equalling in inhumanity those that had taken place in the German concentration camps.

Valour rewarded

Mountbatten came back after the war a hero and was created Earl Mountbatten of Burma. All other Allied countries showered him with honours, too.

His marriage with Edwina was entering a new phase. She had been heavily involved with one man during the war – and suddenly he had announced to her that he was going to marry someone else. Mountbatten supported her through her grief and jealousy, and both were aware that their own marriage benefited from this new closeness.

In 1946, Patricia, Mountbatten's favourite daughter and his confidante, married. In some ways, she was more important to him than Edwina, because he told her everything, and Edwina was often too busy or not concerned enough to listen. The wedding was a grand, typically Mountbatten social event in Hampshire. The King and Queen were there, and for the first time Prince Philip and Princess Elizabeth were photographed together publicly.

The Raj ends

In 1947, Mountbatten was offered the post of Viceroy of India, with the task of 'bringing down the curtain' on the British Raj. It was an awesome responsibility which involved the transfer of power back to a bitterly divided population of 400 million people. He took up his appointment on 24 March 1947 with a 15-month deadline in which to bring about a solution. In typically forthright fashion, he decided it would be better to effect a transition within five months.

Hulton-Deutsch Collection

♛ *A growing rapport developed between the Vicereine and the country she had adopted. The Indians adored her and her mere presence in public ensured a large following. She also developed a deep relationship with Jawaharlal Nehru, the Indian Prime Minister, below, a man for whom Dickie also had the deepest respect and admiration*

Popperfoto

Hulton-Deutsch Collection

Topham Picture Library

♛ *The marriage between Patricia and Lord Brabourne was welcomed by Dickie and Edwina and proved to be a tremendous success. The birth of five grandsons – including Michael-John, seen at his christening in 1950 – was a great consolation for the fact that the couple had had no sons of their own*

♛ *After their return from India, the Mountbattens revived much of the high life they had enjoyed in London before the war. Dickie and his younger daughter Pamela right celebrated the run-up to Christmas 1951 at a ball given in the Savoy. But the pinnacle of Mountbatten's career was to be reached in 1955 far right when, 41 years after his father's resignation from the same job, he was appointed First Sea Lord*

Popperfoto

The dream of a united India, however, proved impossible. Instead, the broad divisions of Hindu India and Muslim Pakistan emerged, along with 500 mini-kingdoms which had to choose to ally themselves with either India or Pakistan. It was an impossible situation, and in the rioting and famine that followed as many as two million people died.

During the time they were in India, Edwina formed her strongest relationship outside her marriage – with Jawaharlal Nehru, the Prime Minister of India. Unlike Edwina's previous affairs, this one was a meeting of minds with a deeply spiritual side, and perhaps not sexual at all. Mountbatten was not jealous – he liked and deeply admired Nehru too, and the men got on very well. He said, without rancour, that the affection of his wife for his friend helped in the difficult task of deciding India's future.

Never in Mountbatten's career had Edwina's help and influence been so evident. She was more than an equal partner while they were in India. She was almost competitive – pushing herself to work even harder than he did in her own particular work, which was relieving the suffering caused in the aftermath of partition. Her work at times was intensely practical – after a riot she was once seen helping to move the piled-up corpses to the mortuary.

At their farewell banquet, Nehru paid tribute to Edwina. 'The gods or some good fairy gave you beauty and high intelligence, and grace and charm and vitality ... they gave you something that was even rarer than those gifts – the human touch, the love of humanity, the urge to serve those who suffer and are in distress ... Is it surprising ... that the people of India should love you and look up to you?'

These were not just words – Edwina loved India and its people, and was loved in return.

Vindication in honour

After the transfer of power had been completed and they had moved back to England, Mountbatten turned down a number of prestigious job offers – such as Ambassador to Washington and Minister of Defence – because this time he was determined to go back to sea. By his own choice, he took a fairly junior position as the commander of the First Cruiser Squadron in the Mediterranean, serving under people he had commanded during the war. Edwina once more threw herself into the work that meant so much to her – with the St John Ambulance Brigade.

In 1955, Churchill appointed Mountbatten First Sea Lord, the position from which his father had had to resign so ignominiously during World War 1. It was what Mountbatten had worked and hoped for – in honour of his father and the family name.

AS TIME GOES BY

The Mountbattens lived life to the hilt. Blessed with Edwina's inheritance and his Royal connections, they were able to enjoy the very best. But their precious possessions also include proud memories of Dickie's glorious career – from his first naval commission to his appointment as Chief of Staff – and cherished souvenirs of the more gracious aspects of domestic life, including priceless heirlooms and touching mementoes of their travels

♔ Dickie received this magnificent Silver Ghost Rolls Royce from Edwina as a wedding present. He loved driving it and soon had the traditional winged mascot replaced by a more personal and distinctive emblem *left*

♔ The *Lion (above centre)* held a special place in Mountbatten's naval career. It was the flag-ship of Admiral Beatty – his hero – and, in 1916, his first commission. But it was the *Kelly (right),* whose command he assumed during World War 2, that will always be associated with him. His leadership inspired intense loyalty and heroism from the crew. *Right* Mountbatten poses proudly with his collection of swords, presented to him on the day he was appointed Chief of Armed Forces in 1958

H. M. S. Lion 1916

♔ The Mountbattens spent happy years in many beautiful homes. In India, they occupied the splendid Viceregal Lodge in New Delhi with its beautiful Moghul Gardens *below left*. Among their many cherished and treasured possessions at Broadlands was the fine Sèvres and Meissen porcelain *below*. When they left Malta in 1954, they were presented with many farewell presents. *Bottom* Pamela holds a bowl made from 400-year-old chestnut wood and Edwina, a perfect model of a Maltese rowing boat, complete to the smallest detail and made by hand

Baron/Camera Press

IN WHICH WE SERVE

EDWINA'S DEATH SHATTERED MOUNTBATTEN, BUT, CHARACTERISTICALLY, HE RALLIED TO ENJOY A BUSY AND FULFILLING RETIREMENT. IRONICALLY, HE DIED AS HE MIGHT HAVE WANTED – AT SEA AND AMONGST HIS BELOVED FAMILY

EDWINA'S HARD WORK EVENTUALLY took its toll. In early 1957, she saw a heart specialist who told her that unless she slowed down, she would be dead within three years. In typical fashion, she merely intensified her efforts.

In 1959, she set out on her last trip, to Ceylon, India and Indonesia on behalf of the St John Ambulance Brigade. In Delhi, she spent a few days with Nehru, although she did not tell him how ill she was.

On 18 February 1960, Edwina flew to Jesselton, North Borneo and, without stopping, began an arduous programme of public duties. The matron at a hospital she visited mentioned that she had tottered with exhaustion and seemed weak and ill. She was found dead in bed on the morning of 21 February.

Mountbatten was woken from sleep to be told of her death on a faint telephone line. For months afterwards, he relived that moment, night after night, in dreams.

Edwina's body was flown back to England and, in a generous gesture, Mountbatten wrote to Nehru and shared the sorrow with him: 'It was quite unbearably moving, the more so as her little sealyham, Snippet, somehow got loose and dashed out of the front door wagging her tail as she always did whenever Edwina came home.'

Mountbatten grieved deeply and long. He forgot all the bad times they had suffered and remembered only the good. This was partly because they had reached a point where it looked as if they had resolved their problems.

'The real tragedy was that we were closer than we had ever been and were getting on marvellously just before she died,' he said. 'We

Weidenfeld Archives

⚓ *The Far East tour Edwina embarked on at the end of 1959 was gruelling by any standards – for a sick woman it was risky in the extreme. The picture above was taken at Jesselton, North Borneo, the day before she died. As head of the St John Ambulance Brigade, Edwina insisted on following the official programme and inspecting a parade of volunteers, despite feeling distinctly unwell*

were looking forward to growing old together because we had everything in common.'

Edwina's funeral was at Romsey Abbey, where six weeks previously Pamela had married David Hicks. She had asked to be buried at sea, and Mountbatten was deeply moved that her coffin was piped aboard the ship at Portsmouth, an honour 'which I have never known to be accorded to any woman other than a reigning sovereign'.

Mountbatten knew that he would never remarry, although some expected him to. He was still a handsome vigorous man, just 60, and was very attractive to women – but no one woman had the qualities that had kept him attached to Edwina through thick and thin. Two years later, he was flattered when a beautiful European princess in her twenties fell in love with him and pursued him doggedly. But he was not for a moment tempted – although he noted in his diary that 'the whole experience was pretty good for the morale'.

Objectives achieved

That first summer after Edwina's death, Mountbatten instituted a new family custom. He kept the whole month of August free to spend with members of the family at Classiebawn Castle, a mansion in County Sligo, Ireland, which Edwina had inherited but they had rarely used. The house itself was not special, but it was near the sea in stunning surroundings and Mountbattens young and old enjoyed the outdoor activities on offer.

Once Mountbatten had recovered from the worst days of his bereavement, he worked harder than ever. In the last five years of his professional life, he threw himself into his ambitious plans to streamline and modernize

Daily Mirror FEB. 22 1960 No. 17,475

TRAGEDY OF 'LADY LOUIS'

She dies, 7,000 miles away, as Royal Family rejoices over the birth of the Prince

'Lord and Lady Louis' at Britain remembers them together...

COURTEOUS MOUNTBATTEN 'Lady Louis' in military uniform.

HER FABULOUS LOVE STORY By Noel Whitcomb CENTRE PAGES

I VISITED THE MOUNTBATTENS AT HOME By Audrey Whiting PAGE ELEVEN

♜ *Top* **Mountbatten, flanked by daughter Patricia and close friend Admiral Sir Charles Lambe, salutes as his wife's coffin is taken aboard HMS** Wakeful *for burial at sea left. The nation's grief gave him some comfort, but Edwina's death was a shattering blow. 'Miserable,' he wrote in his diary. 'I never realized how much I loved her and what she meant to me'*

the Navy, and unify the three ministries of the armed services. By the time he retired in 1965, he was proud that he had succeeded in these objectives.

Retirement, when it came, was only nominal. Mountbatten continued to work vigorously on a voluntary basis right up to his death. He was involved with 179 organizations – for some of which he did an enormous amount of work. Among these he had ties with the Admiralty Dramatic Society, the All England Lawn Tennis and Croquet Clubs, and the Zoological Society, as well as social clubs.

But the organization to which Mountbatten devoted most of his energies in his retirement was the United World Colleges, schools which brought together young people from all over the world. The idea had been Kurt Hahn's, founder of Gordonstoun, the school attended by Prince Philip and his three sons. The first United World College opened in 1962. Mountbatten envisaged a chain of schools whose graduates would grow up without prejudice, tolerant of all nationalities, colours and creeds. He hoped that eventually they would become leaders in their own countries, ruling with trust and goodwill. His over-riding interest, he said, was in 'peace, not education'.

Also during his retirement, he made a 12-part autobiographical series for television: *The Life and Times of Lord Mountbatten*, a fascinating film which took three years to make.

Forthright views

Throughout his life, Mountbatten was never afraid to put forward his point of view. He was horrified by nuclear arms, and campaigned for nuclear disarmament. In a strongly worded letter to *The Times,* he said that the use of nuclear weapons could only end 'in escalation to Total, Global, Nuclear Destruction'.

A LIFE ALONE

It was during his years of retirement that Mountbatten developed his extraordinary relationship with Prince Charles, who looked on him as a grandfather – both his real grandfathers were dead. Mountbatten had already played a vital role in Prince Philip's life, sharing his upbringing and, to a certain extent, orchestrating his romance with the Queen. Both of them were deeply fond of him. They liked and admired him, and would take his advice.

His influence on Prince Charles was profound. When Charles was a child, he looked on Mountbatten as just an adored great-uncle, interesting and very good fun. Mountbatten spotted the little Prince's potential from an early age.

Later, as Charles grew older, they tried to see each other at least once a month. The young Prince would drop in to Broadlands, often bringing his current girlfriend, and the two men would talk for hours. Prince Charles valued his advice above everyone's.

Happy final years

In the early days, it was Mountbatten who helped map out Charles's career. Later, he used his influence in the more personal area of Charles's life. In 1974 he told Charles: 'I believe, in a case like yours, the man should sow his wild oats and have as many affairs as he can before settling down. But for a wife, he should choose a suitable, attractive and sweet-charactered girl *before* she met anyone else she might fall for.'

The major blow in Mountbatten's life was certainly the death of his wife, but it could not dampen his spirits forever. His closest friends, such as Barbara Cartland, remember him for his sense of fun. He made the most of every occasion, and participated wholeheartedly both at work or play. One entry in his diary illustrates this. At the age of 75, he accompanied the Queen to the FA Cup Final at Wembley to watch his local team, Southampton, play. He was not a football fan, and hardly knew anything about the game – but he knew who he supported. When Southampton won, he wrote, 'The whole place went mad, but the Royal Box sat rather glumly, so I stood up by myself and cheered and waved and shouted.'

Everyone who knew him could see that he was a deeply contented, happy man by the end of his life. He had achieved everything he wanted – the legacy of which was that he was perhaps rather vain and self-satisfied, which amused his friends, but may have irritated others. But his family adored him, and the feeling was mutual.

This affection explains why the family were always happy to join him in August at Classiebawn. At dinner on 26 August 1979, his family remember Mountbatten saying: 'I can't think of a more wonderful thanksgiving for the life I have had than that everyone should be jolly at my funeral.'

The next morning brought events that stunned and horrified the world. Just before 11.30 in the morning, six members of the Mountbatten family party set out on a typical adventure. Lobster pots had been set the day before, and they were off in a boat to lift them and see what they had caught. Mountbatten's favourite daughter, Patricia, accompanied him with her husband and 14-year-old twin sons. Patricia's mother-in-law, the 83-year-old

♛ *The elder statesman who had been on such familiar terms with President Kennedy in 1963* top *continued to wield enormous influence in his retirement. The photograph* above, *taken by Norman Parkinson in 1978, shows Mountbatten as an enduringly proud and vigorous man*

♛ *'Prince Charles is an absolute Mountbatten. The real intelligence in the Royal Family comes through my parents to Prince Philip,' Mountbatten claimed mischievously. He encouraged his young protegé to think for himself, and they often argued – fiercely, but always fairly*

CLASSIEBAWN CASTLE

'No place had ever thrilled me more,' Mountbatten wrote of his first view of Classiebawn Castle. The house itself, a neo-Gothic mansion, was rather ugly, but the surrounding countryside was beautiful. From 1960, he and his extended family enjoyed many idyllic summer months there, fishing, setting lobster pots and riding along the beach. The company of his ten 'enchanting' grandchildren was a particular pleasure in his old age. 'It is wonderful to have such a delightful family . . . I am indeed a very lucky person,' he wrote in 1977. Although Mountbatten consulted Scotland Yard before each visit to Classiebawn, and the Irish police mounted a discreet guard while the family was in residence, the threat of kidnap or assassination always seemed remote. With uncharacteristic modesty he remarked, 'Do you really think the IRA would think me a worthwhile target?'

By courtesy of Thames TV plc

♛ *Following Edwina's death, Mountbatten's happiness centred on his family, and their annual Irish holidays. Friends and relatives made a willing crew for his boat,* Shadow V

♛ *News of Mountbatten's assassination passed like a shock wave round the world. On that terrible August day, a total of 18 British soldiers also lost their lives – blown up by an IRA bomb at Warrenpoint*

Dowager Lady Doreen Brabourne, completed the party.

The rest of the houseparty, including Mountbatten's younger daughter, Lady Pamela Hicks, and her husband, had decided not to join them.

They all piled into the boat *Shadow V*, with Mountbatten at the helm, and made for the lobster pots. They were watched by a small crowd of interested sightseers – and a couple of IRA bombers.

At exactly 11.45, there was a huge explosion that tore the boat apart. The IRA had planted a bomb on board. The two bombers had been sitting in an inconspicuous car waiting their moment and activated the bomb by remote control.

The force of the explosion killed one of his grandsons immediately, as well as a young boy whom Mountbatten had allowed to join them on the trip. The old lady was fatally hurt and died some time later. Patricia and her husband had their legs broken as well as other serious injuries. The other twin grandson had injuries to his face and body, but was the least seriously affected.

Mountbatten himself died instantly. The bomb was placed just under where he was standing, and it blew him straight up into the air. Most of his clothes had also been blown off in the blast, but his T-shirt still clung to him in tatters. It was new, designed to commemorate

'I adored him –

and miss him

so dreadfully

now'

PRINCE CHARLES

HMS *Kelly*, and was decorated with the slogan 'The Fighting Fifth'.

Those who knew and loved Mountbatten agreed that in some ways he would have deemed it a perfect death. He died at sea, and was a victim of war of a kind. He was 79 but he was still vigorous and healthy, in full possession of his faculties. One of the things he would have found most difficult to handle would have been a slow decline. But the fact that young people had been killed, and that his adored daughter had been badly injured, made it a disaster that he could not have borne.

The manner of his death ensured the kind of coverage that Mountbatten would have approved. The news made international banner headlines. Tens of thousands of letters from ordinary people were sent to the survivors offering prayers and condolences. Perhaps Mountbatten would have been most touched by the effect of the news in Burma and India. In Rangoon, people queued for four days to sign a book of tribute at the Embassy. In New Delhi, a week's State mourning was declared.

'A very great man'

Prince Charles, who had once said of Mountbatten, 'I admire him, I think, almost more than anybody else. He's a very great man,' was heartbroken. In a simple tribute he said, 'I adored him – and miss him so dreadfully now.'